cloud birds

poems

sheila packa

wildwood river press
duluth, minnesota

Also by Sheila Packa: *The Mother Tongue*
Echo & Lightning

Wildwood River Press
1748 Wildwood Road
Duluth, MN 55804

www.wildwoodriver.com

ISBN 978-0-9843777-2-5

Library of Congress Control Number: 2010935471

Acknowledgments: "Dozen" was published in *Shared Visions*, Calyx Press, 2004. "Between Two Shores" and "Wave" (as "Shadow in the Twilight," a slightly different version) were published in *Trail Guide: Northland Experience in Poetry and Prints*, Calyx Press, 2005. "My Father" and "Across the Border" were published in *Kippis!* Winter 2010. "Not Forgotten" received a poetry award at the Bob Dylan Festival in Hibbing, Minnesota. "I Said I" and "In Translation" appeared in the online poetry journal, *qarrtsiluni*, 2011. "Broken Line" was published in the chapbook, *Love's Cloth*, for the exhibit at the North End Gallery in Superior, Wisconsin, Venus: Poets & Fiber Artists Reflect, 2008. Thank you to the Arrowhead Regional Arts Council and the Loft McKnight Fellowships for past financial support.

Cover design by Kathy McTavish
Visual art © Cecilia Ramon, Refuge, I / Refugio, I (homage to Ana Mendieta) http://www.ceciliaramon.com

*"there are still other songs
magic words learned of,
plucked from the wayside,
broken off from heather,
torn from thickets,
dragged from saplings...."*

The Kalevala

cloud birds

bear

wing

cloud

chosen

I came home
to hear the great grey owl
call into the early dark
beyond the clearing
over the growl and screech
of an animal sheltered
by fallen tree
burrowed out of reach
of talons and beak
below the black tangle
and pine spears
above crystalline snow
and moonlit drift—
a merciless hide and seek
followed by inscrutable silence
near and far
the lift of dark wings
into the old ash and gleam of star
or flame with no in- or exhalation
where wind hauls its ice
and diamonds sift
into the blue night.

spilled
     for ana mendieta

so light
    the trembling of leaves
        in the water's mirror
    shadow of your contour
shoulder on shore
    line of tree your spine
        so dark
    the stones depth cold hip
I trace the root
    in the earth's script
        where you've cast runes
    written yourself in blood
or feathers spilled and mud
    taken up with gunpowder
        returned what never returns
    to the continent or your hands
memory of fire
    that cast its spark
        into the vast body giving birth
    and reaching
the branch that breaks
    beneath the feet
        drew yourself upon a leaf
    falling
from a tree or upper story
    lost with certainty
        the perfect execution—
    self was never the answer
only earth

without the body

an eagle rides the wind
above a ribcage of deer
vertebra fasten into the long grass
of the ditch

without the body
spirit folds like steam or mist

at the center
the wind sings inside
a long loneliness no word can abate

the broad wing-stroke and curved beak
navigate by coordinates

near and far and to her nest
made of sticks and mud and pitch

a small tail feather drifts
upon a spotted fawn hidden in the trees
a wood thrush calls

entrails, marsh marigold, lupine
dandelion fluff, broken glass, blood
flies swarm in the sun

at the wide and narrow gate
where loss hinges on gain

opens into the balance
dissolves like rain

encounter

for the bear
freedom is bound by what it can scavenge
it lives by opportunity
is curious

for a woman in this world
freedom is bound by fear
it has its own body and sound
a distortion

to walk on a dark street
go through some door

once I met my fear
upon the street
once at home under a raised fist
that moment stands on its feet

I pull myself away
make a larger circle
see a life eaten by fear itself
go into cloud, cross the border

to thunder and release
on an unfamiliar road
use the voice
you know it has teeth

sub-boreal

I carry the broken and bent
that lean out from symmetry

sub-boreal cold
bone without marrow

leafless crowns waiting for storm
to come down

narrow gate
into wide fields of cloud cover

shadow after loss
uneven slope
roots in the constellation of star moss

dead fall and beginnings of river
whispers and rifts
steady rain through the night

stones broken from higher
cathedrals where spruce hold
empty nests

glimpses of light
the quiver and bow
and arrow of wild geese

bear

In the forest we cross paths.
Trees shift like a curtain
and a magician in black coat tails
steps into the spotlight.

Fears loom like large boxes on wheels.
I watch darkness in the darkness
take in one breath at the edge
while the other side rolls like a dark sea.

Is this the god that summoned me?

The bear has no sleight of hand
it conceals, reveals
silhouette, dark coat, red sequins, flashing swords.

I heard wings.
We come together for this ceremony
a dove flies up
time stutters, runs both forward and back.

A blade plunges in dark silk
in the hush, an electric solitude.

primitive

in green
in shadow with wide wing spans
on the roots of the oldest melancholy tree
in our own strange garden
deep in bright ferns
in the sunlight of this cathedral space
high near the river's source
join our bodies irrevocably

body of a woman

the body of a woman
has startling darkness
eternal hunger
lives concealed
her vision might blur
but not the sense of smell
she follows not touch
at berry time
her young find what she finds
they come sleeping
during the season of sleep
follow her into deep thickets
up trees
in margins
she becomes fierce
her memory has slashed
the bark of trees

body

the body of a bear
has its own heat and soot
made of fallen stars
coal deep hungers

the body has its own sea
no moon upon the waters
time and tide

the body hides both shadow and light
rises from its tracks
comes to me shaggy and curious

brings its ear
to the silence, tooth and claw
foraging

from the swamp and thicket
river corridor to the door

once I was alone
once I thought my path was never
crossed by magic

spine

this delicate stack
won't collapse
beneath the weight
of sky
this carriage
of linkages
heart and lungs
my own beliefs
on the spine
everything
must balance
made from saplings
and harbors of wings
questions and
clear-ringed breathing
open to wind
without toppling
to flame without
annihilation of fire
built of minerals
and roots
sinew and blood
bending and swaying

spectrum

the bear
is obsidian held fast
inside a mirror
plunged into dark
emanates coal
before diamonds
an aura beyond night
a universe without stars
shining on a shipless sea
without shores

voice

from a scroll of birch bark
fallen leaf
without syntax or vocabularies
from the dark mouth
of the bear with sharp teeth
in vibrations timbers sighs
inside or beside
from wind over and beneath
the bottom of the lake
the burrow and mark
through silence or history
lost or failed
from crows screech _____
a grief

rough tongue

rough tongue, wild one
I woke to you washing me
the friction of your tongue
pulling at my skin

your teeth, dark ivories
capable of biting
it's how we live these days
rasping to each other

I turn my belly to you
throw back my head
in the sun
I could become your prey

but don't
I'm another predator
hungry and sly
can growl and huff and fight

and bolt
for now, I won't—
when you stroke me like this
it almost hurts

red

red has earth in it, blood
in it, the sun and Mars and dreams
iron and grain and grist from the mill
a redbird, a wing feather from a blackbird
redpoll, cardinal, cedar waxwing
a fragrance, heaviness
apple, pepper, persimmon, pomegranate
thorn-apple, high-bush cranberry, rose hips
inside the body in it, fallen pine needles
falling leaves, a bank of coals, fire
and tail lights and stop signs and flags for the mail
resin and amber and lava in its core
bee balm and heirloom roses
tomatoes and hickory and stain
wetness and passion and wool
and rubies and agates—source of rain

following

The black of the bear
is the black of a pupil
which emits no light but takes it in
to the retina.
The encounter of a bear is ocular.
I have never felt, smelled
or touched a bear
only seen some
only heard one bawling.
The others were silent, in motion.

I can't understand time.
If I moved, the past I left
transmitted into photographs
black and white.
As a child, I turned
the black pages of the photo album
to the picture fixed in black corners
of my father's uncle Theodore
and his dog. The dog was nursing
beaver kits.
I keep this moment of love
before his suicide.
Everything changes.

Fear affects the pupils of the eye
emits no light but takes it in
works like a shutter
freezes the image.

My father worked midnights
drove a black Oldsmobile
kicked black tires.
He was smudged with soot
his fingernails stained
with grease, fed me
in the red kitchen chair
fearful stories of bears
only to keep me safe.

Now bears show themselves to me
cross the roads I'm on
enter the field
eat the berries I would eat
turn their heads so that I can see
their ears in silhouette.

I wear black, roam the countryside
love rising in my breast
to face all of them,
the beautiful, fearful bears.
Fifty years and more
I have lived in the north, in the woods
and dreaded what needed love
the emulsion
and source of light
the enduring motion.

absence

I don't have to touch—
it's enough to know
you go into the forest

sleep on the roots
of an unknown tree
wake in a sunlit meadow

you've made your mark
gratitude rises like roots
that cross stones

streams meander along slopes
shadows deepen
we walk on separate paths

cross each other's footprints
hold the silence
whatever falls here falls

into it, whatever springs up
fills it, we abide here without want
flow beside flow

isn't enough

love isn't enough
and desire travels
across the margins
and binding
into another country
and verse
reaches
into the suspension
of dragonfly
and shadow
of hawk and cloud
on the wild rose
and the holy rising up
from the luminous hill

wave

in the twilight of forest
in layers
where limb tangles with limb
under ash trees, inside leaf

green spheres, under fallen
trees with crowns touching ground
around upended roots
through dark trunks into streams

both hollow and crest
rolling over stones
into caverns, around hidden turns
light and deep

season of sleep

below cold drift
excavated winter iron ground
roots and leaves

bear turns in her cave
as bent in the wind boughs rub
until they're worn and break

into blind beginning, she pushes
in the underground womb
vowel without consonant

layered stone with pomegranate
far-fetched honey
red rose camellia

her breath lifts matted fur
tumbling from summer's mate
where rack and friction

finally gasp and glisten
what was not there to give but given
wrapped in the folding

night tied with star's thread deep
scars in crimson arrive
mouths sweet as blessings

honey

in the memory of honey
the door where we kissed
a wave at the window
combing and braiding yellow
orange red blue blossom
white petal black stamen
in the wax
memory of waning
of sunlit spooning
clamber of a small body
drawing the milk down
of walking on cushions
invisible roads
in the memory of palm
of tongue of lips of fingertips
heat and sting
beginning with hunger
ending with sleep
in the memory of clover
you beginning with seed
ending with earth

pine

my home is made of lights
in the pine
it takes my weight
sways when I climb

bends in the wind
when I'm underneath
my home is made of tangles
fruit out of reach

inside are hymns
in the circling of years
in the roots
knives that pierce the stone

need to go that far
to get that deep
water falling clear
made of dark without walls

made of sleep
seeds encased in cones
my home
my berth

wild

an hour of musk
dark fur
an hour of fallen leaves
an hour that is mine I give to you

whatever has not been taken

you fall into sleep
when snow covers the land
and dreams fly south
to new territories

enter the other
world from your den
go in alone
come out as two

your call is a language
I can not speak
that opens a vault
I have no shelter from

what shadow shines
through your being

what burns like a stone
through this life
what have I found?

wrapped in shadow
seeking solitude
alert to new worlds' violent ways

you rise from the tangle of roots
I walk over you

listen to the upward drifting
night
two stars shine on

whatever you are is a gift

wing

memory migration

Across the summers
through corridors of fluttering aspen
and birdsong, I rode a bicycle
along empty roads under a clear sky
crossed by turtles' relentless journeys
towards the ponds and dragonflies
games of tag, dogs chasing
passing cars, entering the funnel cloud
of dust floating above the river
through the pines where birds flit
on the branches building nests
feeding the young, hurrying on to flights
longer and farther across the borders.
The roads had no end, only yearning.
This was the north, the clouds were a language
that cast its shadows on hills, still unpeopled
mornings carried the sounds of trains
history was still coming.

traveling

at night, passing cars' headlights
cast a square of light
that peeled from the window
above my bed and coursed around the room

when I was very small
below my mother's face

wrapped in a yarn tied quilt
two sides of the same stitch
her breath my breath

the light blurred as if it were made
of smoke
with pine branches
etched on its panes

searching the four corners
of my room
before sleep and after
when she was out dancing

dreams cast their bright
green and bounced the light
swished like horse tails
jet streams and sun's

red-gold ignitions
behind the lifted silhouette of wings

taking me
as I lay suspended on the distant music
door after door closed

as one by one the years
peeled off
flew into the wind

my mother
the house the land
other worlds emerged underneath
wore down to a thread

in the coming of age layer after layer lifts
deep lines carved by the past
open like a crevasse
until the frame shifts and falls in

open to sky's brilliant
stream

fluency

When I was small, I had no word for it.
It sifted in the Minnesota woods, in wind
whispering above me in the pine boughs
and waited inside the dark seeds ready

to split their hulls and stand up
like spring, green in the sun.
It sprouted like potatoes
in the cold cellar and in the ground

grazed with all the mares.
It was stacked in the sunlit dust
of the hay barn
and rusted with the car bodies

abandoned in the field
played on the burial mounds
walked over stories kept from me
and slept on the shores of all the lakes.

It rubbed between my immigrant grandmother
who couldn't speak English
and me who couldn't speak Finnish.
It ticked itself from the clock

rose like yeast that lifted the dough
in heat to bread. It wound in the yarn
she slipped with a hook, washed
through all the linens

swelled like the sister
beneath my mother's apron
entered through the pores
of my skin and pushed out as breasts

pumped through my veins
and bled between my legs
slid beneath my skirt and buttoned
in my blouse. It steeped in my cup

floated in the church singing its hymns
repeated its vows in sentences
that trailed off
before too much could be said.

It was the echo of silence
before the storm and after
I heard it nights from inside the walls
later, in the backseats of cars

and from cattail beds
in hawks' wings over the Divide—
where rivers split
into fast tongues.

rapture
"Lucy in the Sky with Diamonds"

north of town by the railway bridge
a man opens the midden heaps
near the tracks south of Biwabik
swinging his metal detector back and forth
over the graves of battered teapots
old bottles of Lydia Pinkham's Home Remedy
looking for silver and gold

nearby the town cemetery
wrought iron gates open
to the grid of sealed graves
beneath a stand of Norways
that give way to the lake
carrying the midnight voices
of teenagers parked in the lanes
sealed inside the cars
without headlights
behind steamed windows
drinking beer, pulling down zippers
shedding jeans like snakes' skins
delirious, urging themselves on
crying, crying, oh!
to be so oblivious to the dead

I think of them now—
voices fluent with life
the call of the train
oh, the many ways we rise

was it I

who drank from
the springs in the headwaters
trampled tradition
escaping the small town
or the mine the men the thefts
joined the union and strikes
or swam through water-filled mine pits
snuck past gates trains conveyors
furnaces beer cans bottle-filled weekends
portaged through chains of lakes
drifted through culverts below railroad tracks
beneath the bridge of language
past locations inebriated
no man no woman no grandchild
of the Divide wanting
lessons from libraries or schools
that came down by arson
not banker or engineer or driver
of cars that rolled in the ditches
not miner with cows or chickens
or cats in the barn
hay cut and put up for winter
not the wife with the pressure cooker
who sealed green beans in the jars
not the gas station attendant or candy store
owner or lifeguard or seamstress
stitching scraps of cloth
not husband or lover or lake
who broke it off seeped in the ground
evaporated
got in the car and kept going

through the streets of rain
free love and tokes of weed and war
and war at the corner
of a movie theater and real
at the corner of never coming back
of dawn and dead of night
of erosion and accretion
through lock and dam
nervous breakdown and exhilaration
listening to broken records old tapes new
at the place where friends desert you
through any channel on any road
through the gutters and sewers
not seeing stars for the light
nor bounds because gorgeous
unrestrained rides of your life
around the bend
was—is within reach
at the edge surging
into waves on the beach
moonlit white capped deep
shadow and silver or tin or stainless
long lines lifting bending
with roots that hold down a city
or a country or the earth
beginning beginning
nothing is as good as the voices
bells ringing in the places
where towers have fallen
lightning and flood now search and rescue
in the rising water broken city
what I took for sunrise

migrations and winds
piercing all I could ask was for more
to carry it through
churning in my wake
wild abandon vibration echo
changing throat and ear
collisions of notes or clouds
pushed by wind and gravity
sideways to go off course
broken faults in stone
see in the sky an opening
to moon through star-scape
give to the last coin and accept
union as grace
if it was an accident never the same
uncover recover gain
over the obstacles
past ordinary stops to the place of sky
no longer with veins or edges
continuous simply leaf and twig
falling shadow given to trees
to someone faraway who comes in pain
turns into waves pounding on shore
unmeasured in its own rhythm
keeping aloft the only part of love
not fixed but divine
given without expectation
pouring from far
river that comes up in all of our feet
falls from our hands
into the loom without frame
weave of sheer or wind or unwinding

velocity

One driver stops in the rain
lifts a broken wing
on the street outside the house.
He moves two ducks
one dead, feathers spilled and floating
across the lanes, one wounded.

Endless traffic flows along the highway
drivers and passengers sealed up
in a hurry, on the phone, distracted
making lists, spilling coffee.

I watch, close to being severed myself.
My grandfather in his grave
plays his violin.
I hear him beneath the ground
playing everything that has fallen
in the leaf mold and black dirt
and silence.

The wounded bird sways
next to the body of its mate.
A woman came
and wrapped the wounded
with a blanket and carried it
in her arms like a baby
gave it back to the water.

My grandfather plays the violin
to nobody who is listening.
He plays to the stones
who say nothing.
He plays to the rivers and to the sky.
Only the lifting wings keep his rhythm.

woman, river

A woman was leaving
the river ran over stones
in its bed, around bends.
He was still sleeping.

It was morning, she
was gathering things into
her suitcase. River was murmuring
but she didn't hear

because the time was near,
she was taking things off her list.
The leaves in the trees
were restless. Rain was coming.

She could only take so much
what she could carry
and wouldn't be missed
A little bit of cash.

She used to play under the bridge
where the water wandered
as if it weren't going anywhere
where sun distilled the leaves into tea

where she had picnics
in the shade. The river combed
the grass, braided her hair
into its current, shook her free.

She touched bottom
put her weight down, closed
the latch. Not a match

the violence.

In its silence the river took
those days out to sea
who knew where
she would cross or when—

the woman next door
knocked and gave her a book
pages torn, repaired with tape
a little something tucked inside

saved her, simply.
She waved from another shore
couldn't say goodbye
made her escape.

door

My mother stood at the counter
tapped an egg
against the rim of the metal bowl
and emptied the broken halves.

Nothing else holds together
with such perfect seamlessness
nor is so fragile.

I was at the table with a box of crayons
watching. I drew a house, a tree
a big sun. She took the whisk to stir
the batter. The door held a secret
every time somebody passed through
something changed.
She bent down to give the little dog a treat.

I was outside, repairing my mascara.
I was bringing home the baby
as she poured batter
on a hot griddle and turned the thin cakes
stacked them on a plate.

We washed the dishes.
Through that door one day
went she, the little dog, my home.

It was never simple
feast or flight.

dozen

I've broken some dreams I've had
those sold by the dozen
that come in a box

perfect in their places, mute.
It gives me a certain pleasure
to choose the right one

and smash it against the metal rim
to pry them open
let the thwarted birds fry

and myself feast.
Even the halved and broken shells
emptied of their jewels, glisten.

between two shores

What is the eagle stealing
as its long wings
grasp and climb the wind
far up in the silence
with two birds chasing?

On the highway
beneath the ascending flights
tangling dark birds in pursuit.

Already too late, already the swaying
shadows fail and outwit the tender watch.

What rides on an eagle's indifferent motion
in the rising thermal currents as the sun glances

off the wide surface of the lake
what waves or sky or emptiness?
What is the news
what wars are beginning
what are the eagles dreaming
as streams tumble down the granite face
break free from the hill, gain flight

grow free

I wait for my sister—
pussy willows then single blades
of green appeared
amid the straw. Next catkins lengthened
on the branches
we walked below. Sometimes between
a bellwort blooms
as we wander through balsam trees.
She is trying to get away.

One day the hawk's gaze
from an overhead wire
fell on me. The next day I found a wing
on the road, broken hinge
bloody bare—after that a rabbit crossed
my path pursued by a wolf into the thicket
neither glanced back.
God speed. Nothing more.

A few days later, I pass another
beheaded rabbit
abandoned to the crows.
We don't imagine the worst, even her.
She doesn't let herself see.
The buds open out into leaves
asparagus rises. I eat the chives'
hollow spears at the table—

a deer followed. My dog finds its sleek hoof.
We go on, amid the evidence
find marsh marigolds at spring streams
new planted trees.
The lilacs bud, we count the blooms.

coffee

My mother lit the burner
beneath the glass coffee pot
on the stove. I could hear the blue flame
water began to bubble
push itself up the slender glass stem
into the glass lid, rain down
into the glass basket, darken the brew.
I set the table, put out a plate of sweets.
Company comes, they leave
the kitchen's dark, then gone.
Forty years have passed.
Nothing's the same
but let's drink some coffee.
We like it dark, even darker.
I like to see it so clear.
Coffee tastes more round
when cooked in the glass percolator.

a question of pomegranate

inside the red fruit
with water flowing over my hands
I found Persephone

swallowing a seed
in a pact with darkness
found sisters, daughters, winters

full of returnings
inside, a question about myth
if a seed splits open and takes root

in the belly
then doesn't every woman bear its fruit?
in every case, misgivings

a seed with the weight of stars
with stars' distance, only deep
stirring the earth's grief

to climb from winter into spring
into tendril and leaf
a seed with a heart of memory

or desire to be spent by light, taken
by dark, spoiled
never the same

a beginning
more beginnings
not healing but flowering

breathe

once I wanted words to become a bridge
built of lost years

the line that holds the sky
upon the water
with concrete pylons sunk deep below the river
lifting to the flight of cranes

wanted words like iron rails to carry freight
as I trembled beneath

but the day they wandered upon the bridge
gazing down
lost in dreams of light
I could not warn them

the boy racing like wind the girl behind
could not save them
unable to find their speed, unable to fling
themselves to safety
brakes smoking burning
in the face of unstoppable violence
they were overtaken, broken, spilled—

words become unspeakable—

so now I disassemble myself
pull away from the sun silvering the tracks
fall into the bloom of algae
erase lines as we watch helpless
upon the same shore—

surrender them to bees, yellow blooms
rafts of lily pads rooted but floating

grandmother rising

my grandmother's heart grows inside my body
into vine and leaf that winds like a wreath
from all the hungers and empty places
from never again

my grandmother's rage in my abdomen
the secrets, the pain
burn like wood rising in a flame
her fires shift in the grate

her hands lift the spindles over the lace
that reached down once to caress my face
for years I've heard the stitching
of her sewing machine

a longing that reached across a border
into a language I couldn't speak—

in translation

the name of the river
has fallen into another river
Zambini-nimi

names are buried by falling leaves
as the next rise from the roots

in your words another people
the settlers displaced

in violence is a silence
a river only has its mouth
never saves itself

we know the boundary
the harbor in each breath
the shores

but not between
in the currents
journey is erased

we carry a map and a book
say these are the stones

cross a bridge into memory
everything here
will be pulled down by gravity

while below
the high water mark
a river gone

isoaiti

in her house long after it's fallen
at the end of a long country road

I pull the chain from the light
touch worn fabric wooden arm
by the kerosene stove

see from window's threshold
limbs that held me when I climbed
and lifting bird's wing
landing from here and there
to the clothesline (sheets taken in)

or roof of a house that turned its face
aside dust and heat sunlit doorway
unzipped rubber boots
on the grit of dark porch stairs
dog barking against

the sound of an old clock ticking
marking quarter hours
water falling in the basin
coffee pot purring
worn thin disintegrating

she uses the flax now flowering
to weave me into her again
gives me blessings of wind
in the trees
lights in the dark
of her hallways

gives me verses in an unknown tongue
lights the star that holds a spark

beginning in silence's furthest gift
follows a broken circle
through the curtains of northern light
gathering planting feeding losing
offers a drink from crimson
roses and stills

a sip of meandering
a cup of smoke
tart raspberries and brandy
birds' intoxications
starlight from a dipper extended

tender palm and perpetual
dreaming pendulum

blizzard

do you hear
how the wind blows, bringing snow
broken trees that block the drive

drifts of toys in childhood mist
from years of Christmas past
easily torn wrap

corkscrew ribbons red curls
cookies piped with frosting
sprinkled with colored sugar

blowing around the eaves
my father's breath, smell
of brandy, my mother's perfume

a house filled with strangers
in another landscape and my own bundle
of baby, pale flannel and pillows

traveling by car and boat
to music, no end to the swaying
crosscurrents and eddies

all slant and upward and down
can I make it into gingerbread
hang the ornaments and tinsel

bring into love's clasp every bite
pull close and hold each winter
open my hand

savor awake before it's lost
or broken, in every circle
ask the bird singing in the cold

its heart, this time a shattered icicle
a snow globe
feast we live inside

amazing how one gift opens
into another and then memory
blows from the northeast

waves turn into snow—
isn't it precisely brief
and long melancholy?

thread

she makes a world tonight
in her hands
small sticks of an unstable loom

seeming mindless under the light
makes a stocking from another unraveling
the broken unused misfit
part of an old skein used yarn

steep wall of language
like a slipped stitch this pain each hole
a line running down to emptiness
to her it doesn't matter

reason for fallen stitches
internal fault
reason for earthquake or malignancy

inattention or accident or mysterious design
unknown lengths
she counts with her fingertips

violent longings
taken with a mild and luminous motion

like many grandmothers begins
increasing at this point on the map
fills her lap
comes to peace using

the only end within reach

broken line

forgive me
if I hurt you
it was an accident
the continuous thread
pulled by my needle
that pierced your skin
drew a drop of blood
that bloomed
like a tear
a tiny strawberry stain
you were sweet
there were rivers
between us
one day I went too deep
had to undo
the seam we made
take out the stitches
start over again

bridge

a black crow flies
then three
into the forest of my grandmother

in the tangles
words of a song she sang
scattered like children
or implements

hay rake pitchfork shovel
disk milk can
cream separator
sold at auction

the wind goes
to the place where she came

where she once held me
where everything was understood
in the circle of her arms
the dog
even a foreign sea

in the field a fallen barn
an empty rib cage of deer
the leaves whisper

of the journey
on the road that turns to bridge

—it's morning on the other side of the world
while I write this
the sun has come up tomorrow

under wing

if she was wing to me
    an arrow in the cloud
if she was eye to me
    and light's vector
if I followed her voice
    climbed in wind before settling
if she was hand to me
    then it was feather
if she was hip then she was tree to me
    as much root as swaying crown
if she couldn't be drawn
    she was vast to me
if her death
    took down the last of her shelter
if I was lifted
    she was blowing northeasterly
if she was lost
    I couldn't dream of her journey
in my canopy
    wrapped by my weavings
if someday you ask why
    or how can it be
I will answer, come fly to me
    and then fly after

peeling apples

In my own kitchen
at the counter
surrounded by apples
I pull off the stem one by one
run my knife blade
beneath the skin
round and round
peel off a spiral of time
come and gone.
This time, the pie is for
my son, his grandmother
who has passed
and the man I'd married
and left, for the family.
Apples always remind me
of hearts. Shorn, they reveal
some bruises.
It was a difficult divorce
but not everything I had feared
happened. It's been
twenty years past.
I cut the apples in half—
then quarters. The tears
I pry out
with the tip of the blade
to be thrown into the compost.
I fill the brown bowl
add the sugar and cinnamon
roll out the pie crust
making a circle
in what will inevitably

be sliced.
I wonder now where
are the lines?
From my oven
the smell of burnt sugar
and apples
sweet and whole.

not forgotten

I learned to ride
the two wheel bicycle
with my father.
He oiled the chain
clothes-pinned playing cards
to the spokes, put on the basket
to carry my lunch.
By his side, I learned balance
and took on speed
centered behind the wide
handlebars, my hands
on the white grips
my feet pedaling.
One moment he was
holding me up
and the next moment
although I didn't know it
he had let go.
When I wobbled, suddenly
afraid, he yelled *keep going—*
keep going!
Beneath the trees in the driveway
the distance increasing between us
I eventually rode until he was out of sight.
I counted on him.

That he could hold me was a given
that he could release me was a gift.

magic

at twilight in early summer
on a road in the country—
I saw a girl standing outside
a run-down farm
in front of the machinery
and yawning dark doorway of a gray barn—
she was wearing
a worn denim jacket
over a long pink ruffled skirt—
staring down at the satin as if
she didn't recognize herself or realize
that her thorny stem
ragged leaves or feet in the dirt
were leading up to one thing, herself
once tightly closed
suddenly with petals, blooming

my father

My father is outdoors
all things everywhere
show the work of his hand
the swing, dog's house
fences around the garden
the tame edge of forest.

He is an engine that throbs
like a tractor.
If I call to him, he won't hear me
he is herding clouds
along the sky, trundling the moon
around in darkness
tying the dogs up for the night.

From the window, I look
into the dark at the edge of light
into silence when the barking dies down.

When we have turned off the lights
except for one on the stove
he will come in. When we are sleeping
when his work is done
he'll take the bread we've made.
Like faith, when we are dreaming

hearing his footstep
him at the table.

in the factory canteen
> painting by Ruslan Andreevich Kobozev

after the shift, cleaned up
he finds a table
in the industrial twilight amid smoke
and fire stacks
gazes at the woman serving
or her tray, the steaming bowl of soup
play of light
he holds a slab of bread

desire—

      she wears a watch
drops her gaze
makes her trades
fills her apron pocket with coins
amid the clatter of spoons and dishes
goes about the tables of men
meets his eyes
with a glass half empty, half full

casualty of the underground mine

the man who lived in a tree
stretched on a limb
in the rain or wind
would not descend

reached into the sky
because he couldn't sleep
for waking

would not mend
because what he lost
would not return

because he had been too deep
and it was difficult to breathe

because there are many ways
to be at home

he could hear the northern lights
he crossed the border for his reasons
the man who lived in a tree
needed rocking of a different cradle

because some things have no language
and what he had to say
needed birds in flight

sheets

washed of the bodies' oils
wet sheets twisted and wound into roses

that filled the baskets my mother
and I once carried from the galvanized tubs
by the wringer and tiny wheels running

in the subterranean darkness
outside to the thirsty air
like promises strung across the span

clipped with wooden spindles
corner to corner
releasing lovers' dreams

that snapped in the wind to fill like sails
above the leaves of grass and fallen pinecones

while the dog went about secret errands
and the cat came with small sacrifices to lay at our feet

line after line of the fabric worn thin
stained with wine or blood
bleached by moonlight and waves
from the fathoms we've crossed

now without her
I pull in sheets from the lilac air
like a fisherman pulling in nets
filled with a catch of sun

banners

I call my garden
what comes up without intention
turn the latch
walk among wild roses
columbine
along the paths of other beings
call what softens the seeds
to be broken from the inside
what bends, unfurls
hoists tiny bells to ring
over the leaves
lifts the weight of air
daisies and fireweed
even though I pull
thistle roots
cut away the deadfall
call gift, the weeds
white blossoms that opened
as we spoke, keep opening

sculpture

perhaps love is borne of stone
that slept in the earth

hewn by a vision
circling the marble's
unknowable dimensions

incited from breath's measures
or instinct

sculpted by hand
knowing fine veins or grain

what emerges
breathes not this air, but another

perhaps love is willingness
to break open the stone

hammer chisel rasp
risk its ruin
make only dust

every measured blow
a force that frees the body
every strike

a call to the other world
to come

unnamed

not the poem
but a topographical map of the body

a carving or summoning
spell or liturgy
a bit of shelter I carry around
so I can sleep in beautiful places

a document of loss
unfinished
sort of a reversed obituary
scratched by a quill or etched like frost

not the poem
the begetting
voices who can't be seen
or the curious light between
letters or lines like rain darkened
tree trunks or stones
split like lightning

cloud

refraction

after ice-out on Crow Lake
when my son was small
muskies came in the bay

from the other world
barred and mud colored
small fins whirring

as they moored their long bodies
near the dock
we lifted the tackle

stared into cold water
to the ribs of lake bottom
through cloud shadows and glancing

surfaces before his father and I
split and divided
dangled in front of the fathomless

bending weeds
and drowned mayflies
the lure on long filament

beside an empty rocking boat
released and reeled
the hook concealed by a minnow's body

into the muskie silence
that clear bright day
over the border

years later
I put my hand in the water
the mirrored one passed through

as if light through light
and the bait suspended
went in came out drifted

in the muskies' open jaws
too ancient or canny to bite
trouble or blessing

love

at first I didn't know
if it was a bell that rang in the church tower
or a parade
a book returned after long absence
or part of myself
half of a prayer
or if it was a war that called us up
or a circle we walked in when we were lost
I didn't know it was a road
that could erase every trace
like a sea that parted
not just any story
that opened and took me in
but one that gathered the shards
of broken glass and set them like diamonds
into a life I didn't know was music

road

I was a road
traveling destinations not my own
an escape, an exit, a promise
bringer of bridges
a story with no clear beginning
or end increased by telling
I was the merging
and lulled plenitude
with semaphore and symbol
amid miles
leading and following
opening and opening
a route of oncoming lights
rain and brakes and radio waves
way of anonymous occupants
lost in reality
crossed by the wild and invisible
not home but alternate
not vision but place of daydream and collision

two worlds

I crossed through a mirror
in one world people were leaving
in the other, arriving

on the other side, the ancestors'
face in mine
as if through a fire's light

spark to tinder, coals to ash
as if through herring in the sea
through memory's country

through clouds to the land
over the border
my name on their stones

words resurface
walk the same walk
under the same stars

footsteps over footsteps
sit at the table sing a hymn
in the old tongue

I go forward and back
return the journey
the road is the road

ten rivers into the Baltic
ten into the inland sea
the longest distance

to the farthest point—
calling to each other
the past and future meet

departure's gift

I hold a thoroughfare
of light falling through the pines
unfolding stripe of shadow

sky etched by cloud

tables filled with leavings
wheat for the bread
strawberries for the jam

paths through houses
gardens that were not my gardens
hands that held me awhile
before moving away

cupboards cannot close it in
mirrors don't reflect
rooms can't contain
paper cannot map
all the things given up

even the body

leaves to the wind
seeds to the field

back ways to fallen barns
where owls call out in the dark

how emptiness comes to the brim

across the border

you arrive
in the stomp and slide
of boots outside
in the papers and boxes and coils of rope
smell of soap
through an open window
in the sound of knives and spoons and forks
but when I look, all the cups
are stacked in a row
and sounds echo
in the chambers and vessels and metals
across borders into music and silence
and then into birds
I find your touch
in wool washed in cold and hung to dry
tracked in my flower beds and snow drifts
and photographs of the old
creameries and camps and co-op houses
know you are passing into other lives
through clouds over the pine horizon
in the sun coming back
into a new life
with silver keys in the mailbox
into the world further and further
on the shore of the seas and in the vapors
to and from a satellite
past the planets
into the papers of books I've yet
to write and translate back
into the language of trees

street musician

you play upon the street
filled with low notes and stones
vibrating slowly, your strings are rivers
rushing down the slope

bird calls from the swamps
strange lights shining afar
ladders that extend
to regions that I wait for

departures, bridges
with loose planks and rivets
you play the tattoo parlor
have stained me without ink

your strings are roads
that connect to the highway
miles I haven't gone
your strings are machines

that run in factories, whistles
that start and stop the work
sirens that scream down the dark
avenue past quick and silent exchanges

by strangers or the light
slowly changing in rooms
glances between people on the street
your strings are the train tracks

going out of town
the cables buried under ground
benches where the homeless sleep
the pier where waves break

and the lonely wait upon the horizon
ships that ply the harbor
veins that hold iron and blood
sinews attaching muscle to bone

the wrenches, pliers
and hammers working
cities upon the same long river
barges carrying freight through lock and gate

prayers that rise up
in the churches and in the bowery
to the clouds moving
as you move your hands

persephone

a journey rises in the palm
   fingers' transculent light
      falls in the direction of sound
         moves aside invisible weights

comes back
   along black stones
      moonlit steps
         through a door without a key

along a river
   from shores of the past
      where moon's pendulum
         spills into waves

by sands
   lit by firmament
      into the wax and wane
         flower of pomegranate and its seed

behind winter's drifts
   to her grief
      on the shore of another continent
         over ranges between

in a seagull's cry
   across the beach where the night wind
      shakes the window
         comes inside the broken

face of an old clock
    rim of a cup
        takes upon the tongue
            desire that never unspoke itself

into silver filigree
    of ash at the edge of the fire
        into red memory
            white hot combustion

through smoke and snow
    over the threshold
        behind the cloth of roses
            as if branch or stitch or leaf might speak

on the narrow boards down on her knees
    unlatch the case
        lift the strap
            enter the instrument

migrations

"in resurrection, there is confusion" H.D.

near shore another story
places that no longer know me
shifting stones of memory

seen and unseen rivers
not knowing whether it's birth
or death

restless wind broken ice shelf
wolves running deer
clouds building towers

between two distant poles
holding back letting go
irresistible winged and dark streams

rising interior maps
north and south
equal opposing

departures unaccounted for
a lone lonely flying over
no longer owned except by wind

or inevitable turning
whether there is a god or
a darkness that draws green leafed

into sky scrawls
along the earth spills into
snowmelt and lake and wing

upward light that draws urge and flight
no matter the form
abandon might take

mirrored in the waters
reversals returning
waves climbing over themselves

resurrecting what goes into root
lost into found, blurred, hungering
surrender

cloud birds

we live on both sides of the border
in two countries
in and outside each other
bone and blood
in disguise without intention or force
without blandishments
blown by wind
silent like shadow crossing and crossing
over the boundaries without end
borne by moon or sun
burnished by wing

opposites

here I love you
along a road where the journey turns back
upon itself

clouds in the sky have no attachment
but search for mountains to the west or
on the other side

amid the rising summer, columbine, daisy, paintbrush
there is the mark of rain
tire track, foot print, bear

the silence is filled with birds
at this moment, we are between green walls
in a double weave
sometimes I fall into a dream in the sunlight

lay my cheek on your shoulder, against muscle
sometimes I climb on your back
and journey into both worlds

find strawberries under the leaves

love travels by foot along two roads

waking

I woke in the night
as an echo
returned part of my life

woke when it came back with light
and trembling of leaves
came back as rain

woke in the farthest place
where we met
above clouds and shadows
in the blue arch

each heart beat a small drum
wound spring dissipating
each moment turning gone

as if a dream
woke in the night

a voice of fox or woman beyond
the trees
washed downstream
given away to the world
or finitude

woke to the near
volatile invisible dark
that creates annihilates
to dying to birthing
to currencies or

weights or measures or forces

woke listening to the trees
a sound drawn back and forth
galaxy or quasar or anti quasar
electron or positron
sun or a giant red star
supernova or grandmother
woke to a siren or nothing

a second life
across deep red chestnut timber
that takes emptiness
to climb up some string
crossing the lines over and back
to a breath
reaching for word after word after word

woke under the veil
at the bottom of the falls
like the stones shattered below
with no idea what or where
each dark threshold crossed
with speed
into dream and free

woke to giving or being torn from or
clouds or drifting or breaking or tumbling

or why
for air for water for earth for fire
not dwelling but moving
is light upon the earth

in green

I live in a chamber
of sound in a garden a field of clover
I live in a frond a fathom a future
in a stem a bow a string
in a breath a bird in its wing

I live on the stairs
under wraps
in books with pages open listening
pouring tea from a pot I once had
into a shadow remembering

in an opening
that won't serve any longer to catch
unfurled streaming yet
trawling the ocean of dark currents
in a storm that had raged so long
I went down

I live in a window-well
in closed spaces on broken eggshells
where I have never been
at crosswalks shops
on a street that goes down to the sea

I live along a path
that tapers into gravel
small stones broken by beginning
reaching back and forth for light
pulling against the weight
of the open sky

in a green that gathers the evening
the way light takes it in
with graves on both sides
on a road with washouts and frost heaves
by wild rose petals lit and red clover
filled with rain

I live in a place I haven't seen
where bottles driftwood
clouds fog the bottom of things
in green the way it quells
the stark stone

enters water on shore
in drifts and blooms
and stem after stem
in endless branching
a green ruinous and full of roses

near the sea in a dream
with magnified stones
drawn through its rippling surface
held in daybreak nightfall
somewhere between

immigrant

the new rose I planted
by the window flings its magenta petals wide

a city rose
in my forest home sings

I noticed its lonely coast
when I watered
wandered deep into its hue
away from the wild ferns
and fallen trees

hidden birdsong out of the blue
and falls

private words like veils
in the rose language
yet one can see through them

falling clear upon the stones
near the stem with its thorns

wheels and horns

silvers more than I can reach
in a history of flames
and petals that turn to wings

I said I

but I meant
the lonely road where I walk
in the forest
not lost but passing through
boundaries

I meant the stones broken and carried
by glacier that came and left
cold that receded into the season's
berries

where we all come
the place of hidden roots
where I put my weight

one wild stem of columbine rises
with its bud
opens into a tiny lantern made from sunset
and unborn strawberries

I said I but I meant morning's heavy mist
rising from the deep lake
to climb the headlands
from the direction of the sun
where hawks fly overhead

I meant the fox who meanders from this side
to the other
following the scent
not hungry but taken into another
appetite

landscape

I turn to go
but am nothing but path
marked by deer hooves
roots rise from the earth
as a tree drops inch by inch
into thickets and gloom
and mushrooms
beneath and through
balsam aspen spruce
beetles and fungi
fed by fire and rain
needles fallen on the feet
of Norway
on the bank of the river
on the bedrock with streams
I lift my arm
but it has turned to limb
branch twig leaf
raise my voice
but it has turned to breath
my words flutter
in the crowns of trees
I call to you like wind

The poems of *Cloud Birds* are a flight through the western shoreline of Lake Superior and the Iron Range of Minnesota. The poems are about bird migration, immigrants and women moving through violence. This work came together under a constellation of the Kalevala, Pablo Neruda, Yannis Ritsos, H.D., Cesar Vallejo, Allen Ginsberg, the myth of Persephone.

Sheila Packa, author of *The Mother Tongue* and *Echo & Lighting,* is the poet laureate of Duluth, 2010-2012. The granddaughter of Finnish immigrants, she grew up on Minnesota's Iron Range. She does spoken word poetry performance with cellist Kathy McTavish and has published poetry, short stories and essays in many literary magazines. Her poems have been in several anthologies, including *Good Poems American Places* (Viking Penguin, 2011) *Finnish-North American Literature in English* (Mellen Press, 2009) *Beloved of the Earth: 150 Poems of Grief and Gratitude* (Holy Cow Press, 2008) and *To Sing Along the Way: Minnesota Women Poets from Pre-Territorial Days to the Present* (New Rivers Press, 2006). Her book of poems, *The Mother Tongue,* published by Calyx Press Duluth in 2007, received a NEMBA honorable mention. She received a Loft Mentor Award in poetry (1995), two Arrowhead Regional Arts Council fellowships for poetry, an ARAC Career Opportunity grant, and two Loft McKnight Awards, (poetry 1986 and prose 1996). Some poems are available in mp3 format on her website, http://www.sheilapacka.com.

Thank you to Kathy McTavish for deep listening. Thank you to Pamela Mittelfehldt for editorial assistance. Thank you to the readers.

CPSIA information can be obtained at www.ICGtesting.com
Printed in the USA

238419LV00004B/170/P